The Woman of Enneagram 4: Love, Marriage, Success Edition

Enneagram For Women, Volume 4

Maria Rondon

Published by Maria Rondon, 2024.

MARIA RONDON
THE WOMAN OF
ENNEAGRAM
4
LOVE, MARRIAGE AND SUCCESS EDITION

THE WOMAN OF ENNEAGRAM 4: LOVE, MARRIAGE, SUCCESS EDITION

First edition. March 28, 2024.

Copyright © 2024 Maria Rondon.

ISBN: 979-8227996756

Written by Maria Rondon.

CONTENT

- The History and Origins of the Enneagram: A brief historical overview of how the Enneagram developed and its relevance to self-knowledge.
- The Importance of Self-Knowledge for Women: Exploring how self-understanding benefits women in various aspects of their lives.

Chapter 1: Love and Creativity

- Bringing Your Creative Vision to Relationships
- Enneagram 4 and Love Compatibility
- How Wings and Subtypes Influence Intimacy

Chapter 2: Finding Your Calling

- Discovering Work That Speaks to Your Soul
- Creative Self-Employment and Entrepreneurship
- Building a Nurturing Work Environment

Chapter 3: Emotional Intelligence

- Tumultuous Depths - Understanding Your Emotions
- Moving Beyond Envy and Melancholy
- Self-Renewal Through Creative Expression

Chapter 4: Wellbeing & Beauty

- The Art of Self-Care and Self-Nurturing
- Finding Beauty in Everyday Life
- Outward Style Reflecting Your Inner Truth

Chapter 5: Conscious Parenting

- Raising Children with Emotional Intelligence
- Fostering Creativity in Children
- Avoiding the Pitfalls of Envy and Resentment

Chapter 6: Spirituality Unbounded

- The Mystical Soul of the Creative
- Connecting to the Divine Through Beauty
- Expressive Spiritual Practices

Chapter 7: Your Wings Explored

- The Influences of Wing 3 and Wing 5
- Integration with Type 1 and Disintegration with Type 2
- Managing Your Wings for Growth

Chapter 8: WORKBOOK

The History and Origins of the Enneagram: A brief historical overview of how the Enneagram developed and its relevance to self-knowledge.

The Enneagram, with its intricate web of lines connecting nine points in a circle, stands as a testament to the human quest for self-knowledge and understanding. Its history, while obscured by the mists of time, is a fascinating journey through human thought, spirituality, and psychology, illustrating our enduring fascination with the complexities of the human psyche.

Tracing the Enneagram's roots demands a foray into the ancient world, where the synthesis of mathematics, philosophy, and mysticism painted a rich tapestry of knowledge. The Greeks, with their profound love for wisdom and the harmonics of the cosmos, laid down the early mathematical and philosophical underpinnings that would centuries later, contribute to the Enneagram's development. It is within the contemplative spaces of monasteries, the dusty scrolls of the desert fathers, and the intricate cosmologies of Sufi mystics, that the Enneagram's symbolic potential began to unfurl.

The transmission of this knowledge into a system for understanding personality, however, awaited the visionary efforts of George Gurdjieff and Peter Ouspensky in the early

20th century. Gurdjieff, a figure shrouded in as much mystery as the Enneagram itself, introduced the symbol as a cosmic map, an emblem of the universe's fundamental laws as mirrored in human consciousness. It was Ouspensky, though, who disseminated the Enneagram's symbolic richness to a Western audience, hungry for esoteric wisdom and self-understanding.

Yet, it was not until the collaborative and innovative work of figures such as Claudio Naranjo, Oscar Ichazo, and Helen Palmer in the late 20th century, that the Enneagram was articulated as a detailed map of personality. Their contributions transformed the Enneagram from a symbol of universal laws into a dynamic tool for self-exploration, linking each of the nine points with distinct personality types, motivations, and patterns of thinking, feeling, and behaving.

This evolution reflects the Enneagram's unique capacity to bridge ancient wisdom with contemporary insights into human behavior. It marries the spiritual with the psychological, offering a pathway to self-awareness that is deeply rooted in the recognition of one's flaws and virtues alike. For women who identify with the Type 4 personality, often characterized by their depth of feeling, introspection, and a sometimes melancholic longing for authenticity, the Enneagram serves as both mirror and map. It offers a language for their inner experiences, a framework for understanding their emotional landscape, and a guide for personal growth.

The Enneagram's journey from ancient symbol to modern psychological tool underscores a timeless human quest: to know oneself. In exploring the origins and development of the Enneagram, we not only uncover a piece of our collective intellectual heritage but also gain insights into the ways in which this ancient system continues to offer relevance and guidance in the pursuit of self-knowledge. As we delve into the intricacies of each type, particularly the nuanced world of Type 4 women, we discover the power of the Enneagram not just as a tool for self-discovery, but as a means of navigating the complex interplay of our emotions, motivations, and behaviors.

The Importance of Self-Knowledge for Women: Exploring how self-understanding

benefits women in various aspects of their lives.

In the realm of personal development and self-awareness, the importance of self-knowledge, particularly for women, cannot be overstated. This pursuit of self-understanding is not merely an exercise in introspection but a foundational step towards empowerment, resilience, and authentic living. The Enneagram, as a system of personality typology, offers a profound framework for this journey, shedding light on the unique paths women can take to embrace their strengths, navigate their challenges, and realize their potential.

The quest for self-knowledge is especially poignant for women, who often navigate complex social, emotional, and psychological landscapes. Understanding oneself deeply—the intricate patterns of thought, the whirlpool of emotions, and the undercurrents that drive behavior—can be a transformative experience. For women, this journey of self-discovery is not just about personal enlightenment; it is about carving out a space in the world where they can stand firmly in their truth, embodying their values and visions with confidence.

The Enneagram, with its nuanced portrayal of personality types, offers a mirror for women to see their most authentic selves reflected back. Each type, with its distinct motivations, fears, and desires, provides a rich tapestry of human experience. For women identifying with Type 4, the Individualist, this journey of self-knowledge takes on a color of deep emotional exploration and the quest for identity and significance. Type 4s are known for their sensitivity, creativity, and an innate sense of uniqueness, but they also grapple with feelings of inadequacy and a longing for what is missing. The Enneagram offers these individuals a language to articulate their inner experiences and a pathway to understand their complex emotions and aspirations.

Self-knowledge empowers women to navigate their relationships with greater awareness and empathy. By understanding their own emotional landscapes, women can foster healthier connections, communicate more effectively, and offer more meaningful support to others. The Enneagram facilitates this by revealing not only how we see the world but also by highlighting how our perceptions differ from those around us. This awareness can bridge gaps in understanding and foster deeper, more fulfilling relationships.

In the professional realm, self-knowledge enables women to align their career paths with their core values and strengths. For women exploring their professional identity, the Enneagram serves as a tool to discern their most fulfilling career trajectories. Understanding one's personality type can illuminate natural talents and potential areas of growth, guiding women towards roles where they can thrive and make meaningful contributions.

Moreover, self-knowledge through the Enneagram can be a source of resilience for women. In facing life's challenges, understanding one's inherent strengths and weaknesses allows for a more adaptive and proactive approach to adversity. For Type 4 women, who may sometimes feel overwhelmed by their emotions, the Enneagram offers insights into managing their emotional intensity and transforming their sensitivities into sources of strength.

In conclusion, the journey toward self-knowledge is a cornerstone of personal development, offering women a pathway to empowerment, fulfillment, and authenticity. The Enneagram, as a tool for understanding the depths of one's personality, plays a crucial role in this journey. It not only aids in the exploration of one's inner world but also enhances relationships, career satisfaction, and resilience. For women, the Enneagram is more than just a framework for self-discovery; it is a guide to living a life that is true to oneself, rich in understanding, and abundant in connection.

Chapter 1:

Love and Creativity

"Bringing Your Creative Vision to Relationships"

In the labyrinthine journey of self-discovery and personal growth, the Enneagram emerges as a beacon of insight, particularly for women identified with the Type 4 personality. These individuals, often referred to as the Individualists, are renowned for their deep wellspring of creativity, emotional depth, and a quest for authenticity. This chapter explores the nuanced interplay between love and creativity, emphasizing how Type 4 women can harness their unique creative vision to enrich their relationships.

Understanding the Creative Heart of Type 4

At the core of Type 4's identity lies a profound yearning for uniqueness and expression. This intrinsic drive stems not merely from a desire to stand out but from a deeper search for identity and meaning through the lens of personal creativity. Recognizing this aspect of oneself is the first step in bringing your creative vision to relationships. It is about acknowledging that your creativity is not just an aspect of your being but a powerful force that shapes how you perceive and interact with the world and those around you.

Channeling Creativity into Emotional Expression

For Type 4 women, emotions are not just feelings but a palette from which they paint the story of their lives. Your ability to feel deeply and intensely can be a gift in relationships, offering a richness of emotional exchange that can deepen bonds. However, the challenge lies in navigating the intensity without becoming overwhelmed. Here, creativity serves as both a conduit and a translator for emotions. Use your creative pursuits—be it writing, painting, music, or any form of artistic expression—as a means to communicate your inner world to your partner. This not only helps in articulating complex feelings but also invites your partner into your innermost emotional landscape, fostering intimacy and understanding.

Incorporating Creativity into Daily Interactions

Bringing creativity into relationships extends beyond the grand gestures and into the minutiae of daily life. It's about infusing creativity into everyday interactions, turning the ordinary into the extraordinary. This could mean creating personalized gifts that capture specific moments in your relationship, writing letters that articulate your feelings in ways spoken words may not, or planning dates that reflect shared interests and passions. The key is to see these acts not as obligations but as expressions of love and creativity, each moment an opportunity to deepen your connection.

Navigating the Challenges: The Shadow Side of Creativity

While creativity is a strength, it also comes with its shadows, especially for Type 4s. The quest for authenticity and the desire to be understood can sometimes lead to feelings of isolation or being misunderstood. In relationships, this can manifest as a fear of being perceived as 'too much' or 'not enough.' It's crucial, then, to cultivate self-awareness and communication. Share your fears and desires openly with your partner, and invite them to share theirs. Embrace vulnerability as a strength, allowing it to be the soil from which deeper love grows.

Creating Together: A Shared Vision

One of the most beautiful aspects of bringing your creative vision to relationships is the potential for co-creation. Engage in creative projects together, whether it's renovating a space in your home, embarking on a photography project, or writing a story. These shared creative endeavors not only strengthen your bond but also create a shared language of love and creativity. It's a way of building something unique to your relationship, a testament to the blend of two individual visions into a unified whole.

The Creative Dance of Love

For Type 4 women, love and creativity are not separate streams but rivers that merge, each enriching the other. Embracing your creative vision within relationships is about more than just sharing your art; it's about inviting your partner into the deepest recesses of your heart, where creativity pulses as the lifeblood of your identity. It's a journey of mutual growth, understanding, and deep connection, where love becomes the canvas, and creativity, the palette with which you paint the story of your togetherness.

"Enneagram 4 and Love Compatibility"

Within the rich tapestry of the Enneagram, the Type 4, or the Individualist, stands out for its depth of emotional insight, artistic sensitivity, and the perpetual quest for authenticity. These traits, while shaping a Type 4's approach to life and creativity, also deeply influence their experiences of love and relationships. The journey of a Type 4 in the realm of love is one marked by a desire for connection that transcends the ordinary, seeking a bond that reflects their unique identity and innermost feelings. This section delves into the nuances of love compatibility for Enneagram Type 4 women, exploring how their distinctive qualities interact with those of other types to weave the fabric of relationship dynamics.

Type 4s in Love: The Quest for Authenticity and Connection

For Type 4 women, love is not a superficial exchange but an intimate dance of souls. They yearn for a partner who not only understands their complex inner world but also values their uniqueness and depth. This longing for authenticity in relationships means Type 4s are often drawn to individuals who share their appreciation for emotional depth and who are not afraid to explore the shadowy depths as well as the luminous heights of human experience.

Compatibility with Other Types: The Interplay of Hearts

The intricate nature of Type 4s often finds complementary harmony with certain Enneagram types, while with others, it may require conscious effort to bridge differences. Compatibility, in the realm of love, is less about finding an identical match and more about the mutual willingness to understand and grow alongside one another.

Type 4 and Type 2 (The Helper): This pairing can create a deeply nurturing relationship, where Type 2's natural inclination to care and offer support harmonizes with Type 4's desire for understanding and emotional connection. However, the key to balance lies in ensuring that Type 4's need for authenticity and personal space is respected, preventing Type 2's sometimes overly accommodating nature from stifling the relationship's growth.

Type 4 and Type 5 (The Investigator): This combination offers a fascinating blend of emotional depth and intellectual exploration. Type 5's analytical and curious nature can provide a grounding influence for Type 4's emotional intensity, while Type 4 adds a layer of emotional richness to Type 5's world. The challenge here is in navigating Type 5's need for independence and Type 4's desire for emotional intimacy, requiring open communication and understanding.

Type 4 and Type 9 (The Peacemaker): The tranquil and accepting nature of Type 9 can be a balm to Type 4's sometimes turbulent emotional landscape. Type 9's ability to remain unperturbed and supportive offers a stable foundation for Type 4 to explore their creativity and emotions freely. The potential pitfall in this pairing is Type 9's tendency to avoid conflict, which might clash with Type 4's need for authenticity and addressing issues head-on.

Fostering Growth and Understanding in Love

For Type 4 women, the path to fulfilling relationships is paved with self-awareness and the courage to be vulnerably authentic. Recognizing one's tendencies, such as the penchant for idealizing relationships or dwelling on what's missing rather than what's present, allows Type 4s to navigate love with greater clarity and purpose. Embracing the beauty of their emotional depth while also cultivating resilience against the lows of idealization can open the door to healthier, more balanced relationships.

In love, as in creativity, Type 4 women are called to weave a tapestry of connection that honors their deepest truths while also embracing the imperfections and complexities of shared human experience. The journey of love compatibility for Type 4 is not about finding someone who completes them but rather someone who complements their rich inner world, offering a canvas for the mutual creation of a love that celebrates both individuality and union. Through this dance of compatibility, Type 4 women can find not just love but a reflection of their deepest selves in the heart of another, making every moment of connection a masterpiece of their shared creativity and emotional depth.

"How Wings and Subtypes Influence Intimacy"

The Enneagram's depth and complexity offer more than just a static view of personality types; it provides a dynamic framework for understanding the nuances of human behavior and relationships. Particularly for Type 4 women, known as the Individualists, the concept of wings and subtypes plays a crucial role in shaping their approach to love, intimacy, and creativity. This segment delves into how these elements of the Enneagram influence Type 4 women's connections with others, offering insights into the intricate dance of intimacy.

The Influence of Wings on Type 4's Approach to Love

Wings are the adjacent types on either side of a person's core Enneagram type, and they can significantly affect how that core type is expressed. For Type 4 women, the wings are Type 3 (The Achiever) and Type 5 (The Investigator), each bringing its own flavor to the Type 4 personality.

Type 4 with a 3 Wing (4w3): This subtype often embodies a blend of Type 4's depth of feeling and Type 3's ambition and drive for success. In relationships, 4w3s may seek partners who not only understand and accept their emotional richness and need for authenticity but also share their desire for achievement and recognition. Their approach to intimacy combines a quest for deep emotional connection with a yearning for shared goals and achievements. However, the challenge for 4w3s lies in balancing their need for emotional authenticity with their desire for external validation, striving to ensure that their relationships are not unduly influenced by societal expectations of success.

Type 4 with a 5 Wing (4w5): Individuals with this wing are often characterized by a marriage of Type 4's emotional depth with Type 5's intellectual curiosity and introspective nature. In love, 4w5s crave connections that are both emotionally profound and intellectually stimulating. They seek partners who can journey with them into the realms of both heart and mind, appreciating their need for solitude and reflection as well as their intense emotional expressions. The challenge for 4w5s is to open themselves to the vulnerability of intimacy without retreating into the safety of intellectualization or isolation.

The Role of Subtypes in Shaping Intimacy

Subtypes, determined by dominant instinctual variants (Self-Preservation, Social, or Sexual), further refine how Type 4 women experience and express intimacy.

Self-Preservation 4s: Often concerned with issues of security and well-being, Self-Preservation 4s may approach relationships with caution, seeking partners who provide a sense of safety and stability. Their challenge is to balance their need for security with their desire for emotional depth and authenticity, learning to trust that vulnerability can coexist with safety.

Social 4s: This subtype is attuned to the dynamics of social interaction and belonging. In relationships, Social 4s look for partners who understand their complexity and can navigate the social world with them. They face the challenge of balancing their need for social connection with their fear of losing their individuality within the relationship.

Sexual 4s: Driven by a desire for intensity and deep connection, Sexual 4s seek partners with whom they can explore the depths of intimacy and passion. Their challenge lies in managing the intensity of their desires without overwhelming their partners or sacrificing their own authenticity for the sake of connection.

Embracing the Dance of Intimacy

For Type 4 women, understanding the influence of wings and subtypes on their approach to love and intimacy offers a roadmap for navigating relationships with greater awareness and compassion. It encourages an exploration of how their unique blend of emotional depth, creativity, and personal identity shapes their connections with others. By embracing the nuances of their personality, Type 4 women can engage in the intricate dance of intimacy with grace, fostering relationships that honor their profound capacity for love and creativity. Through this journey, they not only discover the richness of connection with others but also deepen their understanding and acceptance of themselves.

Chapter 2:

Finding Your Calling

"Discovering Work That Speaks to Your Soul"

In the journey toward personal and professional fulfillment, the quest to find work that truly resonates with one's innermost being is a profound endeavor, especially for Type 4 women. These individuals are often characterized by their search for meaning, authenticity, and self-expression in all facets of their lives. This chapter explores the depths of what it means for Type 4s to uncover careers that not only align with their profound sense of identity but also enable them to make meaningful contributions that mirror their unique perspectives and rich emotional experiences.

The Soul's Calling: A Quest for Meaning

For Type 4 women, engaging in work transcends the traditional definitions of a career. They seek roles that allow them to leverage their creativity, connect genuinely with others, and introduce beauty and depth into their surroundings. The challenge frequently encountered is how to align the yearning for significant, soulful work with the practical demands of the professional sphere.

Self-Exploration and Vocation

Embarking on a path to discover one's true calling necessitates deep introspection and heightened self-awareness, principles deeply rooted in the wisdom of the Enneagram. For Type 4s, this involves an honest embrace of their uniqueness while consciously navigating their inclination towards idealism, which may obscure their route to fulfilling employment. It's about finding harmony between striving for authenticity and embracing the practicalities of a career.

Cultivating Your Unique Gifts and Talents

Type 4 women are endowed with a myriad of skills and gifts, ranging from artistic prowess and profound emotional insight to an innate grasp of human nature. Acknowledging and harnessing these talents is crucial in the quest for meaningful work. Type 4s flourish in settings where authenticity is cherished, whether this is in the realm of art, therapy, literature, or any domain that prizes originality and depth.

Passion and Purpose as Cornerstones

In the professional lives of Type 4s, passion and purpose are not just concepts but the foundation of their work ethos. Aligning their careers with their passions enables Type 4s to connect with something larger than themselves, offering a sense of purpose that elevates their daily tasks. This may manifest in pursuing roles that have a direct positive impact on others, contributing to societal change, or partaking in creative endeavors that enrich the world.

Towards Authenticity and Alignment

Finding work that resonates with one's soul is also a journey toward living authentically and in alignment with one's true self. For Type 4 women, this entails seeking environments and roles that reflect their core values and allow for the expression of their genuine selves. It involves navigating the balance between ideal aspirations and tangible realities, learning to move through the professional landscape without losing touch with their personal vision and values.

A Journey of Meaning and Impact

Uncovering work that truly speaks to the soul is an exploratory process marked by courage, introspection, and self-discovery. For Type 4 women, it is not only a search for professional satisfaction but for a deeper connection with their identity and life's purpose. By embracing their individuality, recognizing their inherent gifts, and following their passions, Type 4s can find careers that not only resonate deeply but also contribute significantly to the fabric of society. Through this process, the Enneagram acts as a beacon, shedding light on their personalities and guiding them toward a career path filled with creativity, authenticity, and profound emotional understanding.

"Creative Self-Employment and Entrepreneurship"

In the nuanced journey of self-discovery and the quest for fulfilling work, Type 4 women, with their deep reservoirs of creativity and emotion, are often drawn to paths less traveled. The allure of creative self-employment and entrepreneurship holds a special promise for them—a promise of autonomy, authenticity, and the freedom to express their unique visions. This chapter explores how Type 4 women can navigate the waters of creative self-employment and entrepreneurship, transforming their innate talents and passions into sustainable careers.

The Call to Authenticity in Work

For Type 4 women, the conventional career path often feels stifling, a constraint on their authenticity and individuality. The entrepreneurial journey, with its inherent flexibility and potential for personal expression, offers an enticing alternative. It is a path that not only allows for the pursuit of passions but also demands a deep alignment with one's true self. The challenge and beauty of entrepreneurship for Type 4s lie in its demand for authenticity at every step, from the inception of a business idea to the daily tasks of running a venture.

Navigating the Emotional Landscape of Entrepreneurship

Entrepreneurship is not for the faint of heart, and for Type 4s, the emotional highs and lows can be particularly pronounced. The key to thriving in this environment is mastering the art of emotional resilience. Type 4 women must learn to channel their emotional depth and sensitivity into their work, transforming potential vulnerabilities into strengths. This involves developing a robust support system, practicing self-care, and learning to navigate the inevitable challenges and setbacks with grace and creativity.

Leveraging Creativity as a Business Asset

The creative prowess of Type 4 women is a potent asset in the entrepreneurial world. In industries saturated with sameness, their ability to see the world differently and to create from a place of depth and authenticity can set their ventures apart. Type 4 entrepreneurs excel in fields where innovation and originality are prized, from the arts and design to marketing and branding. The challenge is to maintain a balance between creative freedom and the practical demands of running a business, ensuring that their ventures are not only expressive but also viable.

Building a Brand That Reflects Your True Self

For Type 4 women, their business and brand are deeply personal extensions of themselves. Building a brand that truly reflects their values, aesthetics, and unique perspective is essential. This authenticity resonates with customers and clients, creating a loyal community that values the genuine connection and depth Type 4s bring to their work. The process of brand-building challenges Type 4 entrepreneurs to articulate and communicate their vision clearly, a task that requires introspection, clarity, and courage.

Embracing the Journey of Self-Employment and Entrepreneurship

The path of creative self-employment and entrepreneurship is a journey of continuous self-discovery and growth. For Type 4 women, it is an opportunity to live and work in a manner that is deeply aligned with their core selves. It requires not just creativity and passion but also discipline, resilience, and a willingness to learn from both successes and failures.

Crafting a Career That Sings to the Soul

For Type 4 women, creative self-employment and entrepreneurship offer a pathway to professional fulfillment that deeply resonates with their quest for authenticity and self-expression. By embracing their unique talents and perspectives, navigating the emotional ups and downs of entrepreneurship, and building brands that truly reflect who they are, they can create careers that not only fulfill their professional ambitions but also sing to their souls. In this endeavor, the Enneagram serves as a guiding light, offering insights into their strengths and challenges and supporting them in their journey towards creating work that is not just a job, but a true expression of their deepest selves.

"Building a Nurturing Work Environment"

In the evolution of a Type 4 woman's professional journey, the creation of a nurturing work environment is not just a preference but a necessity. This chapter explores the significance of cultivating a workspace that resonates with the deep-seated values and emotional landscapes of Type 4 women, facilitating not only their creative expression but also their personal and professional growth. The Enneagram, with its profound insights into the human psyche, provides a framework for understanding how Type 4s can create and thrive in environments that honor their unique blend of sensitivity, creativity, and authenticity.

The Essence of a Nurturing Work Environment

For Type 4 women, a nurturing work environment goes beyond the physical space—it's about cultivating an atmosphere that supports emotional well-being, encourages authentic expression, and values creativity. Such environments provide the emotional depth and aesthetic harmony that Type 4s crave, allowing them to fully engage with their work in a meaningful way. It's an environment where vulnerability is seen as strength, individuality is celebrated, and the pursuit of personal projects is encouraged.

Creating Emotional Harmony

Understanding and managing the emotional currents of the workplace is crucial for Type 4s. They thrive in settings where emotional intelligence is valued, and where open, honest communication is the norm. Implementing regular check-ins, creating spaces for sharing personal and professional challenges, and fostering a culture of empathy and support can significantly contribute to a nurturing work environment. For Type 4 women, leading or being part of a team that values emotional connectivity and mutual support is immensely fulfilling.

Fostering Aesthetic and Creative Expression

Aesthetic surroundings and the freedom to personalize workspaces can greatly impact the productivity and well-being of Type 4 women. Encouraging the incorporation of personal touches—whether through art, music, or decor—transforms the workspace into a source of inspiration. Additionally, fostering a culture that values creative input and innovative thinking in projects and problem-solving processes allows Type 4s to contribute in ways that feel deeply rewarding.

Cultivating Professional Growth and Personal Development

A nurturing work environment for Type 4s also focuses on opportunities for growth, both professionally and personally. Workshops, training sessions, and mentorship programs that focus on developing creative skills, emotional intelligence, and leadership capabilities can be particularly beneficial. Type 4 women flourish in environments where there is an emphasis on continuous learning and where their journey towards self-actualization is supported and encouraged.

Balancing Autonomy with Collaboration

While Type 4s value their independence and the space to work on projects that resonate with their personal vision, they also recognize the importance of collaboration. Creating a balance between autonomous work and collaborative projects allows Type 4 women to express their individuality while also being part of a community. It's about building a work culture where autonomy does not mean isolation but rather provides the freedom to explore personal creativity within a supportive collective framework.

A Symphony of Support, Creativity, and Growth

For Type 4 women, building a nurturing work environment is akin to composing a symphony where each element—emotional harmony, aesthetic expression, personal growth, autonomy, and collaboration—plays a crucial role. Such an environment not only supports their well-being and productivity but also aligns with their inherent need for depth, meaning, and authenticity in their work. Through the Enneagram's insights into the unique characteristics of Type 4 personalities, we can better understand and implement the principles of creating workspaces that not only nurture the individual but also enrich the collective fabric of the professional landscape. In doing so, Type 4 women can transform their workplaces into sanctuaries of creativity, empathy, and personal fulfillment.

Chapter 3:

Emotional Intelligence

"Tumultuous Depths - Understanding Your Emotions"

Embarking on the journey of emotional intelligence is akin to navigating the vast and tumultuous depths of the ocean for Type 4 women, the Individualists of the Enneagram. With their rich emotional landscapes and innate sensitivity, understanding and managing their emotions is not just an aspect of personal growth but a pivotal component of their path to self-actualization. This chapter delves into the complex emotional world of Type 4s, offering insights into how they can harness their emotional depth for greater self-understanding, resilience, and fulfillment.

The Rich Emotional Tapestry of Type 4s

Type 4s are distinguished by their acute emotional awareness and capacity for deep feelings. Their emotional experience is nuanced and expansive, ranging from the heights of ecstasy to the depths of despair. This intensity of emotion, while a source of creativity and empathy, can also lead to feelings of melancholy and isolation. For Type 4s, understanding their emotional nature involves acknowledging this duality as a strength, not a vulnerability.

Navigating Emotional Waters with Awareness

The first step in mastering emotional intelligence for Type 4s is developing an acute awareness of their feelings. It's about recognizing the triggers that precipitate emotional responses and understanding the underlying needs or desires these emotions signify. Journaling, mindfulness practices, and reflective meditation can serve as powerful tools for Type 4s to observe and articulate their emotional experiences without judgment.

The Role of Self-Acceptance and Authenticity

At the heart of Type 4's emotional journey is the quest for authenticity and self-acceptance. Embracing their emotional depth and idiosyncrasies without succumbing to self-criticism is crucial. This acceptance allows Type 4s to engage with their emotions more constructively, viewing them as indicators of their true selves rather than imperfections. It encourages a compassionate self-dialogue that fosters resilience and a balanced emotional state.

Emotional Regulation and Resilience

While Type 4s naturally experience emotions more intensely, learning to regulate these emotional responses is essential for their emotional intelligence. Techniques such as cognitive behavioral strategies, breath work, and grounding exercises can help Type 4s manage overwhelming emotions and prevent them from dictating their reactions. Cultivating resilience involves recognizing that while they cannot always control their emotions, they can control their responses to them.

Harnessing Emotions for Creative and Relational Depth

One of the unique gifts of Type 4s is their ability to channel their emotions into creative expression and forge deep, meaningful connections with others. By understanding and embracing their emotional experiences, Type 4s can transform their feelings into art, literature, music, or any form of expression that resonates with their inner world. Similarly, their emotional depth enables them to empathize with others on a profound level, enriching their relationships and fostering genuine connections.

The Journey to Emotional Mastery

For Type 4 women, mastering emotional intelligence is a journey of embracing their complexity, navigating their emotions with awareness, and cultivating resilience. It's about transforming their tumultuous depths into a source of strength, creativity, and connection. Through this process, Type 4s not only achieve greater self-understanding and fulfillment but also become beacons of authenticity and emotional depth in a world that often shies away from the full spectrum of human emotion. In this endeavor, the Enneagram serves not only as a map of their emotional landscape but also as a guide towards harnessing their emotional intelligence for a richer, more authentic life.

"Moving Beyond Envy and Melancholy"

The journey toward emotional intelligence for Type 4 women involves navigating through the complex emotions of envy and melancholy, which are often seen as defining aspects of their experience. These feelings, while challenging, are also gateways to profound personal growth and self-awareness. This chapter explores strategies for Type 4s to transcend these emotions, harnessing their depth for a richer understanding of themselves and a more fulfilling life.

Understanding Envy and Melancholy in Type 4s

Envy and melancholy are emotions that arise from Type 4s' intense desire for authenticity and significance. Envy stems from the perception that others possess qualities, achievements, or circumstances that Type 4s feel are missing in their own lives. Melancholy, on the other hand, is often a reflection of their deep longing for an idealized, unattainable reality. Recognizing these emotions as natural components of their emotional landscape is the first step toward moving beyond them.

Reframing Perspectives: The Power of Gratitude

One of the most effective ways for Type 4s to transcend envy and melancholy is through the practice of gratitude. By actively acknowledging and appreciating what is present in their lives, Type 4s can shift their focus from what is lacking to the abundance that exists around them. This practice helps reframe their perspective, fostering a sense of contentment and reducing feelings of envy.

Embracing the Present Moment

Type 4s often dwell in the realm of what could be, which fuels their feelings of melancholy. Embracing mindfulness and the present moment encourages a deeper engagement with life as it is, rather than as they wish it to be. Techniques such as meditation, mindful breathing, and grounding exercises can help Type 4s anchor themselves in the present, alleviating the weight of melancholy.

Cultivating Self-Compassion

The path through envy and melancholy is also paved with self-compassion. Type 4s can be harsh critics of themselves, amplifying their feelings of inadequacy. Learning to treat themselves with kindness, understanding, and compassion is vital. This means acknowledging their feelings without judgment and offering themselves the same empathy they extend to others. Self-compassion workshops, journaling about positive qualities, and therapy can be valuable tools in this process.

Exploring Creative Outlets

For Type 4s, creativity is not just a hobby—it's a lifeline. Channeling their emotions into creative expression provides an outlet for envy and melancholy, transforming them into art, music, writing, or any form of creativity that resonates with them. This process not only allows for emotional catharsis but also affirms their identity and value, counteracting the roots of envy and melancholy.

Building Meaningful Connections

Isolation can magnify feelings of envy and melancholy. By actively seeking and nurturing meaningful relationships, Type 4s can find reflection, validation, and connection. Engaging in communities that share their values and interests, whether in person or online, provides a sense of belonging and reduces the sense of being fundamentally different or flawed.

A Journey of Transformation

For Type 4 women, moving beyond envy and melancholy is a journey of transforming their deepest challenges into sources of strength. By practicing gratitude, embracing the present, cultivating self-compassion, exploring creativity, and building connections, Type 4s can navigate their emotional depths with greater resilience and insight. This process not only enhances their emotional intelligence but also leads to a more authentic, fulfilled life. Through the wisdom of the Enneagram, Type 4s can understand these emotions not as obstacles but as integral to their path toward self-discovery and personal growth.

"Self-Renewal Through Creative Expression"

For Type 4 women, the journey of emotional intelligence unfolds with a profound connection to creativity. Their inherent depth of feeling and keen introspection find a vibrant outlet in creative expression, serving as both a mirror and a map for navigating their inner world. This chapter delves into the transformative power of creative expression as a means of self-renewal for Type 4 women, exploring how engaging in artistic endeavors can foster emotional growth, resilience, and a deeper sense of self-understanding.

The Vital Role of Creativity in Type 4's Emotional Landscape

Creativity is not merely an activity for Type 4s; it is a fundamental aspect of their identity and a crucial mechanism for emotional processing. The act of creating allows Type 4 women to externalize their intense feelings, transforming abstract emotions into tangible forms. Whether through painting, writing, music, or any other creative outlet, Type 4s can explore the nuances of their feelings, gaining insights into their emotional complexities and triggers.

Creative Expression as a Pathway to Self-Discovery

The journey of self-discovery for Type 4 women is deeply intertwined with their creative pursuits. As they delve into their art, they engage in a dialogue with their innermost selves, uncovering hidden aspects of their personality, desires, and fears. This process of creative exploration acts as a reflective practice, enabling Type 4s to understand themselves more fully and to articulate aspects of their experience that might otherwise remain elusive.

Transmuting Emotional Pain into Creative Power

One of the most remarkable aspects of Type 4s' creative expression is their ability to transmute emotional pain and melancholy into art. By channeling their feelings of sadness, longing, and even envy into their creative work, Type 4 women can transform their emotional challenges into sources of strength and inspiration. This alchemical process not only alleviates their own suffering but also resonates with others, offering solace and understanding to those who encounter their work.

Fostering Resilience Through Artistic Endeavors

Engaging in creative expression provides Type 4 women with a resilient foundation to withstand life's emotional storms. The act of creating instills a sense of accomplishment and purpose, countering feelings of inadequacy and self-doubt. Moreover, the creative process requires patience, perseverance, and a willingness to confront and work through challenges—qualities that fortify Type 4s' emotional resilience.

Building Connections Through Shared Creativity

Creative expression also opens avenues for Type 4 women to connect with others on a profound level. Sharing their art allows them to communicate their inner world in ways that words cannot capture, fostering deep connections with those who resonate with their expression. Collaborative creative projects can further enrich these connections, providing opportunities for mutual understanding and emotional support.

The Healing Power of Creative Expression

For Type 4 women, the path to emotional intelligence is beautifully illuminated by the light of creative expression. As they navigate the depths of their emotions through their art, they embark on a journey of self-renewal, transforming their emotional vulnerabilities into sources of strength and insight. Creative expression becomes a sanctuary—a place where they can be authentically themselves, explore the vast landscape of their emotions, and emerge with a renewed sense of resilience and understanding. Through this process, the Enneagram's wisdom serves as a guiding star, offering Type 4 women the insights needed to harness their creativity as a tool for emotional growth and self-renewal.

Chapter 4:

Wellbeing & Beauty

"The Art of Self-Care and Self-Nurturing"

For Type 4 women, the path to wellbeing and the appreciation of beauty are deeply interwoven with the practices of self-care and self-nurturing. These practices are not mere acts of indulgence but essential strategies for maintaining their emotional, physical, and spiritual health. In a world that often feels overwhelming and discordant, creating a sanctuary of care and beauty for oneself is a profound act of self-love and resilience. This chapter explores the nuances of self-care and self-nurturing as art forms that Type 4 women can master, enriching their lives with depth, beauty, and wellbeing.

Embracing the Uniqueness of Personal Self-Care

Type 4 women possess a unique perspective on the world, deeply valuing authenticity and individual expression. This perspective extends to their approach to self-care and nurturing. What works for one person may not resonate with another, making it vital for Type 4s to explore and identify practices that truly speak to their hearts and needs. Whether it's through artistic creation, nature walks, journaling, or meditation, the key is finding activities that nourish their souls and affirm their individuality.

Creating Rituals of Beauty and Self-Nurturing

For Type 4s, beauty is not a superficial concern but a profound source of inspiration and comfort. Integrating beauty into self-care practices can transform mundane routines into rituals of self-nurturing. This might involve creating a serene and aesthetically pleasing environment at home, indulging in skincare routines that feel luxurious and nurturing, or wearing clothes that express their unique style and mood. By surrounding themselves with beauty, Type 4 women can uplift their spirits and cultivate a deeper sense of self-love.

Navigating Emotional Wellbeing with Grace

The emotional intensity of Type 4 can sometimes lead to periods of melancholy or overwhelm. Incorporating emotional self-care practices into their daily routines is crucial for navigating these waters. This might include setting aside time for introspection, engaging in therapy or counseling, and practicing mindfulness and emotional regulation techniques. Recognizing the need for emotional care and addressing it with kindness and understanding allows Type 4 women to maintain their emotional equilibrium and resilience.

Prioritizing Physical Health as a Foundation for Wellbeing

While Type 4s are often drawn to the emotional and spiritual aspects of self-care, recognizing the importance of physical health is equally vital. Regular exercise, nutritious eating, and restful sleep are foundational elements of self-care that support emotional and mental health. By treating their bodies with care and respect, Type 4 women can enhance their overall sense of wellbeing and vitality.

Cultivating Spiritual Connections and Inner Peace

For many Type 4 women, a sense of connection to something greater than themselves is a vital component of self-nurturing. Cultivating spiritual practices—whether through organized religion, personal spirituality, or connection with nature—can provide a sense of peace, purpose, and belonging. These practices can be a source of comfort and guidance, offering a broader perspective on life's challenges and beauties.

The Lifelong Journey of Self-Care and Nurturing

Self-care and self-nurturing for Type 4 women are much more than temporary respites from the demands of the world; they are essential practices that sustain their emotional, physical, and spiritual wellbeing. By embracing the art of self-care, Type 4s can navigate their lives with greater resilience, joy, and authenticity. This chapter is a reminder that in the pursuit of self-understanding and growth, the practices of self-care and nurturing are not selfish but fundamental acts of kindness toward oneself. Through these practices, Type 4 women can create a life that is not only survivable but flourishes in beauty, depth, and wellbeing, guided by the insights and wisdom of the Enneagram.

"Finding Beauty in Everyday Life"

For Type 4 women, the quest for beauty is not merely an aesthetic endeavor but a profound journey towards finding meaning, connection, and solace in the tapestry of everyday life. The Enneagram's rich history and philosophical depth provide a backdrop for understanding how Type 4s can cultivate an eye for beauty in the mundane, transforming their daily experiences into sources of inspiration and wellbeing. This chapter explores practical and soulful ways Type 4 women can harness their innate sensitivity to beauty, turning everyday moments into opportunities for enrichment and self-discovery.

The Essence of Beauty in the Mundane

Type 4s possess a unique ability to perceive beauty in places others might overlook. This capacity is a gift that enables them to find joy and wonder in the simplicity of daily life. By consciously attuning themselves to the beauty around them—from the texture of morning light streaming through a window to the intricate patterns of nature on a walk—Type 4s can create a reservoir of inspiration that fuels their creativity and soothes their soul.

Cultivating Mindfulness to Enhance Perception

Mindfulness practices are instrumental for Type 4s in their pursuit of finding beauty in the everyday. Engaging in mindfulness encourages a state of presence that heightens their awareness of the subtle nuances of their environment. This could be as simple as savoring the flavor of a meal, noticing the warmth of a shared smile, or being moved by the melody of a street performer. These practices not only enrich their appreciation of beauty but also anchor them in the present moment, mitigating tendencies toward melancholy and longing.

Creating Rituals Around Beauty

For Type 4 women, integrating beauty into their daily routines can transform mundane tasks into rituals of self-care and joy. This might involve setting a beautiful table for meals, arranging a workspace with objects that inspire, or curating playlists that elevate their mood. By infusing their day with intentional acts of beauty, Type 4s not only nurture their aesthetic sensibilities but also cultivate a sense of sacredness in their daily lives.

The Role of Artistic Expression

Artistic expression is a natural extension of Type 4s' search for beauty in the mundane. Whether through writing, painting, photography, or music, creating art allows Type 4s to capture and communicate the beauty they perceive in everyday life. These creative endeavors offer a pathway for translating fleeting moments of beauty into enduring works of art, fostering a deep sense of fulfillment and connection with the world.

Embracing Imperfection as Beauty

An essential aspect of finding beauty in everyday life for Type 4s involves embracing imperfection. Recognizing the inherent beauty in the flawed and the incomplete challenges the idealized notions of beauty that Type 4s might yearn for. This acceptance not only broadens their appreciation of beauty but also aligns with their quest for authenticity, allowing them to find beauty in the most unexpected places and moments.

A Lifelong Journey of Discovery

For Type 4 women, the pursuit of finding beauty in everyday life is a lifelong journey of discovery, enrichment, and self-care. It is a practice that nourishes their soul, ignites their creativity, and anchors them in the richness of the present moment. By embracing their natural inclination towards beauty, cultivating mindfulness, creating rituals, expressing themselves artistically, and learning to appreciate imperfection, Type 4s can transform their everyday experiences into a wellspring of beauty and wellbeing. Through this process, the Enneagram serves as a guide, illuminating the path towards a life that not only seeks beauty in all its forms but also celebrates the unique lens through which Type 4 women perceive the world.

"Outward Style Reflecting Your Inner Truth"

In the landscape of Type 4 women's journey toward self-understanding and authenticity, the expression of their inner truth through outward style holds a place of paramount importance. For these individuals, fashion and personal style are not mere adornments but profound manifestations of their identity and emotional landscape. This chapter delves into how Type 4 women can craft an outward style that resonates with their inner truth, turning personal style into a canvas for self-expression and a mirror of their deepest selves.

The Intimacy of Style

For Type 4 women, style is an intimate language of self-expression that communicates their complex inner world to the outside. It's an art form where creativity, emotions, and personal narrative converge to tell a story that is uniquely theirs. Embracing their style becomes a journey of self-discovery, where each choice of color, texture, and form reflects aspects of their personality, moods, and artistic sensibilities.

Authenticity in Expression

The cornerstone of Type 4 women's style is authenticity. In a world that often promotes conformity, daring to stand out with a personal style that is true to one's self is both an act of courage and a declaration of identity. It involves exploring and understanding one's preferences deeply, beyond the influence of current trends, and aligning style choices with the values and aesthetics that resonate most deeply. This authenticity in expression not only empowers Type 4 women but also inspires those around them to embrace their uniqueness.

Emotional Resonance and Style

Emotional resonance plays a critical role in how Type 4 women approach their style. They are naturally drawn to pieces that evoke a strong emotional response, whether it be a sense of nostalgia, joy, or inspiration. This emotional connection to their wardrobe allows them to navigate their often turbulent inner world, using style as a tool for mood regulation and self-soothing. In this way, clothing and accessories become more than just items of fashion—they are talismans that carry personal significance and emotional energy.

Evolving Style as a Reflection of Growth

Just as Type 4 women are on a continuous journey of self-evolution, so too is their style. It is dynamic and evolving, reflecting their personal growth, changing moods, and the shifting landscapes of their lives. Embracing this fluidity in style challenges the notion of a static identity, allowing Type 4 women to explore different facets of themselves and express the richness of their personality in full spectrum. This evolution in style is celebrated as a reflection of their journey toward self-realization and emotional maturity.

Integrating Style and Wellbeing

Ultimately, the integration of style and wellbeing for Type 4 women is about more than aesthetics—it's about creating harmony between the inner and outer self. When style aligns with personal truth, it enhances self-esteem, fosters a positive body image, and contributes to overall wellbeing. This alignment encourages Type 4 women to walk through the world with confidence and grace, fully embodying their identity and embracing their uniqueness.

The Art of Authentic Style

In crafting an outward style that reflects their inner truth, Type 4 women engage in an artful practice of self-expression and authenticity. This practice is a testament to their journey toward embracing their individuality, navigating their emotional depths, and expressing their nuanced identities to the world. Through their style, they invite others into the rich emotional landscape of their inner world, offering a glimpse of their soul's essence. In this way, the Enneagram serves as a guide, illuminating the path toward a deeper understanding of self and enabling Type 4 women to manifest their inner truth through the beauty and authenticity of their outward style.

Chapter 5:

Conscious Parenting

"Raising Children with Emotional Intelligence"

In the realm of conscious parenting, Type 4 women embark on a profound journey, leveraging their innate emotional depth and introspective capabilities to nurture their children's emotional intelligence. This chapter delves into the strategies and insights that can guide Type 4 mothers in cultivating an environment where emotional intelligence is fostered, allowing their children to grow into emotionally aware, resilient, and empathetic individuals. The principles of the Enneagram offer a foundational understanding of self and others that is invaluable in this endeavor, providing a unique lens through which Type 4 women can approach parenting with consciousness and depth.

Understanding Emotional Intelligence in Children

Emotional intelligence encompasses the ability to recognize, understand, manage, and use emotions in positive ways to communicate effectively, empathize with others, overcome challenges, and defuse conflict. For children, developing emotional intelligence is crucial for building healthy relationships, achieving personal goals, and navigating the complexities of social interactions.

Modeling Emotional Awareness and Expression

As Type 4 women are naturally attuned to the nuances of their emotional landscape, they are uniquely positioned to model emotional awareness and expression for their children. By openly discussing their feelings, naming their emotions, and demonstrating healthy ways of expressing them, Type 4 mothers can teach their children the value of emotional honesty and the strength in vulnerability. This modeling encourages children to view their emotions as natural and important parts of their experience, rather than aspects to be feared or suppressed.

Creating a Safe Emotional Space

A cornerstone of raising children with emotional intelligence is the creation of a safe emotional space where children feel free to express their feelings without judgment. Type 4 mothers can nurture this space by actively listening to their children, validating their emotions, and offering empathy and understanding. This supportive environment fosters trust and openness, enabling children to explore their emotions and develop the confidence to express themselves authentically.

Encouraging Empathy and Sensitivity

With their inherent empathy and sensitivity, Type 4 women can guide their children in developing empathy for others. This can be achieved through discussions about feelings, teaching perspective-taking, and encouraging acts of kindness. By helping their children understand and empathize with the emotions of others, Type 4 mothers can instill a deep sense of compassion and connectedness, essential components of emotional intelligence.

Fostering Resilience Through Emotional Regulation

Teaching children how to regulate their emotions is vital for building resilience and emotional intelligence. Type 4 mothers can equip their children with tools for emotional regulation, such as deep breathing techniques, mindfulness practices, and constructive ways of dealing with disappointment and frustration. These skills empower children to manage their emotions effectively, navigate challenges with grace, and maintain a sense of inner calm in the face of adversity.

The Gift of Emotional Intelligence

For Type 4 women, the journey of conscious parenting and fostering emotional intelligence in their children is both a challenge and a profound gift. It is an opportunity to impart essential life skills that will serve their children well into adulthood, enriching their relationships, enhancing their wellbeing, and enabling them to lead lives of emotional depth and understanding. Through the wisdom of the Enneagram and the lens of Type 4's emotional richness, mothers can raise children who are not only emotionally intelligent but also deeply connected to the world around them with empathy, resilience, and authenticity. In this endeavor, Type 4 women find a resonant expression of their own deepest values and a continuation of their journey towards self-discovery and growth, illuminated by the guiding light of the Enneagram.

"Fostering Creativity in Children"

Within the framework of conscious parenting, Type 4 women hold a unique position to nurture and foster creativity in their children. With their natural inclination towards emotional depth, aesthetic appreciation, and self-expression, Type 4 mothers are ideally suited to recognize and cultivate the creative spark in their offspring. This chapter explores the ways in which Type 4 women can support their children's creative development, creating an environment that encourages exploration, imagination, and the free expression of ideas. Drawing on the insights of the Enneagram, this guidance aims to empower Type 4 mothers to guide their children toward fulfilling their creative potential.

Creating an Environment That Inspires Creativity

The foundation of fostering creativity in children lies in creating a stimulating environment that encourages curiosity and exploration. Type 4 mothers can achieve this by filling their home with a variety of materials that spark creativity, such as art supplies, musical instruments, and books across diverse genres. Equally important is the creation of spaces that invite calm and concentration, offering children a sanctuary where their imaginations can flourish.

Modeling Creative Expression

Children learn by example, making it crucial for Type 4 mothers to actively engage in their own creative pursuits. By observing their mothers navigate the realms of artistic expression, problem-solving, and personal projects, children internalize the value of creativity. This modeling teaches them that creativity is not just an activity but a way of viewing and interacting with the world.

Encouraging Exploration and Experimentation

One of the greatest gifts a Type 4 mother can give her child is the freedom to explore and experiment without fear of judgment or failure. This involves embracing the creative process as much as, if not more than, the final product. Encouraging children to try new things, take risks, and view mistakes as opportunities for learning fosters a resilient and inventive mindset.

Nurturing Emotional Intelligence Alongside Creativity

For Type 4 mothers, the nurturing of creativity is deeply intertwined with the development of emotional intelligence. By encouraging their children to express their feelings through creative outlets, Type 4 women can help their children understand and manage their emotions effectively. This dual focus on creativity and emotional intelligence equips children with a rich toolkit for self-expression and empathy.

Providing Opportunities for Creative Learning

Expanding beyond the confines of home, Type 4 mothers can seek out and provide opportunities for their children to engage in creative learning experiences. This might include classes in the arts, visits to museums and galleries, participation in community projects, or attending performances that broaden their cultural and artistic horizons.

Fostering a Culture of Appreciation and Constructive Feedback

In fostering their children's creativity, Type 4 mothers can cultivate a culture of appreciation and constructive feedback. Recognizing and celebrating their children's creative efforts reinforces their sense of self-worth and encourages continued exploration. At the same time, offering gentle guidance and constructive feedback helps children refine their skills and understand the value of perseverance and improvement.

Cultivating Creative Spirits

For Type 4 women, fostering creativity in their children is a natural extension of their own quest for expression and authenticity. By creating an environment that values imagination, modeling creative engagement, encouraging exploration, and nurturing emotional intelligence, Type 4 mothers can guide their children toward a life rich in creative fulfillment. Through these efforts, they not only enhance their children's lives but also deepen their own understanding and practice of conscious parenting, as illuminated by the timeless wisdom of the Enneagram. This journey of nurturing creativity is not just about developing skills or talents but about enriching the soul and expanding the horizons of what it means to live a truly expressive and meaningful life.

"Avoiding the Pitfalls of Envy and Resentment"

In the nuanced journey of parenting, Type 4 women face the distinctive challenge of navigating their deep feelings of envy and resentment. These emotions, if not addressed, can inadvertently affect the parenting dynamic, influencing the emotional and psychological development of their children. This chapter seeks to explore the roots of these feelings within the Type 4 personality and offers strategies for transforming these emotions into opportunities for growth and deeper connection with their children. Drawing from the ancient wisdom of the Enneagram, this guidance aims to help Type 4 mothers cultivate a parenting approach that is mindful, compassionate, and emotionally intelligent.

Understanding the Roots of Envy and Resentment

For Type 4 women, envy often arises from a perceived lack of something in themselves or their lives, coupled with the belief that others possess that desired quality or situation. This feeling can be exacerbated in parenting when comparing their children's achievements or behaviors with those of others, leading to feelings of inadequacy or resentment. Recognizing that these emotions stem from their inner narratives and unmet needs is the first step toward addressing them constructively.

Fostering Self-Compassion and Acceptance

Cultivating self-compassion is vital for Type 4 mothers in counteracting the harshness of self-judgment that envy and resentment can breed. Practicing self-compassion involves acknowledging one's feelings without criticism, understanding that imperfection is part of the human experience, and treating oneself with the same kindness one would offer a friend. Through self-compassion, Type 4s can begin to heal the parts of themselves that feel incomplete or inadequate, reducing the intensity of envy and resentment.

Celebrating Individuality Within the Family

Type 4 women thrive on authenticity and individuality, and embracing these values within their family can mitigate feelings of envy and resentment. This involves recognizing and celebrating the unique qualities and achievements of each family member, including themselves, without comparison. Encouraging each child to pursue their interests and passions, and showing appreciation for what makes them special, reinforces a sense of value and belonging that transcends external comparisons.

Constructive Communication and Emotional Expression

Open and honest communication about emotions is essential for Type 4 mothers in avoiding the pitfalls of envy and resentment. This includes expressing their feelings in a healthy and constructive manner, as well as encouraging their children to do the same. By modeling emotional honesty and vulnerability, Type 4s can foster an environment where feelings are respected and addressed, rather than suppressed or ignored.

Seeking Support and Community

Navigating the complexities of envy and resentment can be challenging, and seeking support from partners, friends, or a community of like-minded parents can provide valuable perspectives and encouragement. Engaging in support groups, therapy, or Enneagram workshops can offer Type 4 women tools and strategies for personal growth, as well as a sense of solidarity and understanding from others who share similar experiences.

Transforming Envy and Resentment into Growth

For Type 4 women, conscious parenting involves a deliberate effort to transform the potentially destructive energies of envy and resentment into forces for personal growth and deeper familial bonds. By understanding the roots of these emotions, practicing self-compassion, celebrating individuality, communicating openly, and seeking support, Type 4 mothers can navigate their parenting journey with grace and authenticity. The Enneagram, with its deep insights into personality dynamics, serves as a guiding light on this path, offering Type 4 women the wisdom to embrace their challenges as opportunities for transformation and to foster a family environment where emotional intelligence, understanding, and love prevail.

Chapter 6:

Spirituality Unbounded

"The Mystical Soul of the Creative"

For Type 4 women, spirituality is not confined within the walls of dogma or tradition; it is a boundless exploration of the self, the universe, and the intricate connections between the two. This chapter delves into the mystical dimensions of Type 4's creativity, exploring how their innate depth, emotional intensity, and quest for authenticity forge a unique spiritual path. The Enneagram, with its ancient roots and profound insights into the human psyche, serves as a map for Type 4 women navigating the spiritual journey inherent in their creative expression.

The Intersection of Creativity and Spirituality

For Type 4 women, creativity is a spiritual act; it is their way of touching the divine, of translating the ineffable into form. This creative process is deeply meditative and reflective, often serving as a conduit for spiritual insights and revelations. Whether through art, music, writing, or any other form of expression, Type 4s experience creativity as a sacred dialogue with something greater than themselves—a dialogue that nourishes their soul and deepens their understanding of the world.

Embracing the Mystical in the Mundane

Type 4 women possess the unique ability to perceive the mystical in the mundane. They see beyond the surface of everyday life, identifying symbols, patterns, and meanings that others might overlook. This perception imbues their spiritual journey with a rich tapestry of symbolism and synchronicity, allowing them to find spiritual significance in ordinary moments. By cultivating this awareness, Type 4s can transform their daily experiences into a continuous stream of spiritual discovery and wonder.

The Role of Emotional Depth in Spiritual Exploration

The emotional depth characteristic of Type 4 women is a powerful tool in their spiritual exploration. Their capacity to feel deeply, to dwell in the complexities of the human heart, provides a fertile ground for spiritual growth and introspection. Emotions, even those that are challenging or painful, are embraced as essential components of their spiritual path, offering insights into the self and the nature of existence. Through their emotional experiences, Type 4s engage in a profound process of transformation, where vulnerability becomes a strength and a gateway to transcendence.

Navigating the Spiritual Path with Authenticity

Authenticity is the cornerstone of Type 4 women's spirituality. Their journey is marked by an unwavering commitment to truth, to aligning their outer lives with their innermost convictions and values. This authenticity demands courage and self-awareness, as Type 4s confront the shadows and illusions that obstruct their path. Yet, it is through this commitment to authenticity that they find liberation and a deeper connection to the spiritual essence of their being.

Fostering Connection and Community

While the spiritual journey of Type 4 women is deeply personal, it is also enriched by connection and community. Sharing their insights, experiences, and creative expressions with others who are on similar paths can provide a sense of belonging and mutual understanding. These connections serve as mirrors, reflecting the shared human quest for meaning and belonging, and reinforcing the idea that while their journey is unique, they are not alone in their search for spiritual depth.

The Creative as a Spiritual Voyager

The mystical soul of the creative, as embodied by Type 4 women, is a testament to the intertwining of spirituality and creativity. Their journey is a testament to the power of embracing one's depth, engaging with the world with a sense of wonder, and pursuing authenticity at all costs. Through their creative and spiritual explorations, Type 4 women not only discover deeper aspects of themselves but also contribute to the collective understanding of what it means to be human. The Enneagram, with its ancient wisdom, serves as a guide on this journey, offering insights and affirming the value of the individual path in the vast landscape of human spirituality.

"Connecting to the Divine Through Beauty"

For Type 4 women, the pursuit of beauty transcends the aesthetic, serving as a profound path to connecting with the divine. This chapter delves into the spiritual dimension of beauty and how it serves as a bridge between the soul of Type 4 women and the mystical. Drawing from the rich traditions and insights of the Enneagram, this exploration highlights the intrinsic link between the quest for beauty and the desire for a deeper spiritual connection. It is through beauty that Type 4 women find not only a reflection of the divine in the world around them but also a means to express their own divine nature.

Beauty as a Reflection of the Divine

Type 4 women possess an innate sensitivity to beauty, viewing it as a manifestation of the divine in the material world. For them, beauty is not confined to visual aesthetics but is present in all forms of expression—art, music, literature, and nature. By engaging with beauty, Type 4s tap into a sense of the sublime, experiencing moments of transcendence that remind them of a greater reality beyond the physical realm. This connection reinforces their belief in a universe imbued with meaning and purpose, where beauty acts as a signpost to the divine.

The Role of Creativity in Spiritual Expression

Creativity is the vessel through which Type 4 women explore and express their spirituality. The act of creating is, for them, a sacred dialogue with the divine, a process through which they can channel and manifest spiritual truths. Whether through painting, writing, composing music, or any other creative endeavor, Type 4s use their artistic expressions as a form of prayer or meditation, a means to commune with the divine and share that connection with the world.

Cultivating Beauty in Daily Life

Integrating beauty into daily life allows Type 4 women to maintain a constant connection to the divine. This practice can be as simple as curating their living spaces with objects that evoke beauty, engaging in rituals that celebrate the beauty of the mundane, or seeking out experiences that fill their souls with awe. By consciously surrounding themselves with beauty, Type 4s create a living environment that reflects their inner spirituality and nurtures their connection to the divine.

The Healing Power of Beauty

For Type 4 women, beauty also holds a healing power, offering solace and comfort in times of emotional turmoil. Encounters with beauty can provide a sense of peace and well-being, lifting their spirits and reminding them of the goodness in the world. This healing aspect of beauty is essential for Type 4s, helping them to navigate the depths of their emotions and find balance and harmony in their spiritual journey.

Fostering Spiritual Growth Through Beauty

Engaging with beauty is not a passive experience for Type 4 women but an active pursuit of spiritual growth. By seeking beauty in all its forms, they embark on a journey of self-discovery and expansion, learning to see the world, and themselves, through the lens of the divine. This pursuit encourages them to develop qualities such as gratitude, mindfulness, and compassion, deepening their spiritual practice and their connection to the divine.

Beauty as a Path to the Divine

For Type 4 women, the exploration of beauty is a spiritual practice that enriches their lives and deepens their connection to the divine. By viewing beauty as a reflection of the divine, integrating it into their daily lives, and using it as a means of creative and spiritual expression, they forge a path that is uniquely theirs. The Enneagram, with its ancient wisdom, serves as a guide on this journey, offering insights into the soul of Type 4 women and their mystical quest for connection through beauty. In this pursuit, beauty becomes more than just an aesthetic ideal—it becomes a way of living, a means of perceiving the world, and a pathway to the divine.

"Expressive Spiritual Practices"

In the spiritual journey of Type 4 women, expressive spiritual practices offer a profound way to navigate their inner landscape, connect with the divine, and manifest their unique essence in the world. This chapter explores the myriad ways in which Type 4 women can engage in expressive spiritual practices that resonate with their deep sense of identity, creativity, and emotional depth. Drawing on the rich tapestry of the Enneagram's wisdom, these practices are presented as avenues for Type 4 women to explore their spirituality in ways that are authentic, transformative, and deeply personal.

Journaling as a Spiritual Practice

Journaling stands out as a powerful expressive spiritual practice for Type 4 women. Through the written word, they can articulate their innermost thoughts, emotions, and spiritual experiences, creating a sacred space for self-reflection and dialogue with the divine. This practice allows Type 4s to explore their feelings and thoughts without judgment, offering clarity, insight, and a deeper understanding of their spiritual journey.

Art as a Pathway to the Divine

For Type 4 women, art serves as a direct conduit to the divine, allowing them to express their spirituality in visual, auditory, or kinetic forms. Whether it's painting, sculpture, music, or dance, engaging in artistic creation becomes a meditative act, a form of prayer, and a celebration of the divine presence within and around them. Through art, Type 4s can transcend the limitations of language, communicating their spiritual insights and connections in ways that are profoundly personal and universally resonant.

Nature as a Spiritual Sanctuary

The natural world offers Type 4 women a boundless source of inspiration, beauty, and spiritual connection. Spending time in nature, whether it's a forest, a garden, or the seashore, can become an expressive spiritual practice. In the rhythms and patterns of nature, Type 4s find metaphors for their own inner processes, seeing reflections of the divine in the intricate beauty of the natural world. This connection fosters a sense of oneness with the universe and a deep appreciation for the sacredness of life.

Rituals and Ceremonies

Creating and participating in rituals and ceremonies provides Type 4 women with a structured yet deeply expressive way to honor their spiritual path. These practices can range from simple daily rituals, like lighting a candle or offering gratitude, to elaborate ceremonies that mark significant life transitions or spiritual milestones. Through ritual, Type 4s can manifest their inner world in the outer, embodying their spirituality in acts of beauty, reverence, and intention.

Contemplative Practices

Contemplative practices such as meditation, prayer, and mindfulness offer Type 4 women a quiet yet profound way to connect with their spirituality. These practices encourage a stillness of mind and heart, allowing Type 4s to listen deeply to their inner voice and the whispers of the divine. In the silence, they find not only solace and peace but also insights and inspiration that fuel their expressive spiritual journey.

The Unbounded Nature of Expressive Spirituality

For Type 4 women, expressive spiritual practices are not merely activities but vital aspects of their being that weave together their creativity, emotional depth, and quest for meaning. By engaging in these practices, Type 4s embark on a spiritual journey that is richly textured, deeply personal, and endlessly transformative. The Enneagram, with its ancient roots and psychological insights, offers a guiding light on this path, affirming the value of expressive spirituality as a means to explore the self, connect with the divine, and express the unique beauty of the Type 4 soul. In this unbounded exploration, spirituality becomes an art form—a profound expression of the mystical soul of the creative.

Chapter 7:

Your Wings Explored

"The Influences of Wing 3 and Wing 5"

In the journey of self-discovery through the Enneagram, the concept of "wings" plays a crucial role in providing a nuanced understanding of personality dynamics. For Type 4 women, the adjacent types—Type 3, The Achiever, and Type 5, The Investigator—serve as wings, offering additional layers of complexity and variation to their core personality. This chapter delves into how the influences of Wings 3 and 5 manifest in the life of a Type 4 woman, shaping their motivations, fears, and behavior patterns. Drawing on the historical and philosophical depth of the Enneagram, we explore how these wings contribute to the unique tapestry of the Type 4 personality.

Type 4 with a Wing 3 (4w3): The Aristocrat

Type 4 women with a 3 wing embody a fascinating blend of the Type 4's depth of feeling and the Type 3's ambition and drive. This combination gives rise to the "Aristocrat" persona, marked by a unique confluence of creativity, efficiency, and a desire for recognition.

Creativity Meets Ambition: The 4w3 woman harnesses her creative energy not just for self-expression but also for achieving tangible success. Her artistic pursuits are often accompanied by a strategic approach to ensure her talents are recognized and appreciated.

Image-Consciousness: The influence of the 3 wing adds an acute awareness of image and how one is perceived by others. The 4w3 woman carefully curates her public persona, blending authenticity with a mindful presentation of self that aligns with her goals.

Navigating Emotion and Achievement: At times, the 4w3 might struggle with balancing her emotional depth with the desire for achievement. This tension can lead to periods of introspection, where the quest for authenticity and success are reconciled in the pursuit of personal and professional fulfillment.

Type 4 with a Wing 5 (4w5): The Bohemian

In contrast, the Type 4 woman with a 5 wing embodies the "Bohemian" archetype—a blend of the Type 4's introspective depth and the Type 5's intellectual curiosity and detachment.

Intellectual Exploration: The 4w5 woman is characterized by a profound intellectual curiosity, delving into the realms of philosophy, psychology, and spirituality. Her creative expression is often informed by an eclectic body of knowledge, making her work rich and multi-dimensional.

Emotional Intensity and Detachment: The presence of the 5 wing introduces a paradoxical blend of emotional intensity and a need for detachment. The 4w5 navigates this by seeking solitude and space for reflection, allowing her to process her emotions and thoughts in depth.

The Quest for Identity: The combination of Type 4's search for identity and Type 5's pursuit of knowledge creates a unique path for self-discovery. The 4w5 woman explores her place in the world through both emotional and intellectual lenses, seeking a coherent sense of self that encompasses her complex inner world.

Embracing the Wings

For Type 4 women, understanding the influence of their wings—whether 3 or 5—provides invaluable insights into their personality, offering a richer perspective on their strengths, challenges, and paths to growth. The interplay between the core characteristics of Type 4 and the qualities of their wings shapes their journey towards self-awareness, creative expression, and personal fulfillment. By embracing the qualities of both their wings, Type 4 women can navigate their emotional landscapes with greater balance, harness their creative and intellectual potentials, and engage with the world in ways that are both authentic and impactful. The Enneagram, with its ancient roots and depth of insight, serves as a guiding light in this exploration, affirming the beauty and complexity of the Type 4 personality and its adjacent influences.

"Integration with Type 1 and Disintegration with Type 2"

The Enneagram's dynamic nature not only encompasses the influence of wings but also the paths of integration and disintegration, which reveal the complex interplay of growth and stress within each type. For Type 4 women, these paths illuminate the transformative journey towards self-improvement and the potential pitfalls during times of stress. This chapter explores how Type 4s experience integration with Type 1, The Reformer, during periods of growth, and disintegration with Type 2, The Helper, under stress. Understanding these dynamics provides Type 4 women with deeper insights into their personal development journey, guided by the ancient wisdom of the Enneagram.

Integration with Type 1: The Path to Self-Discipline and Purpose

As Type 4 women move along their path of integration towards Type 1, they embody the best qualities of The Reformer, channeling their emotional depth and creativity into constructive and purposeful action. This integration marks a period of personal growth where the often turbulent emotions of Type 4 are balanced by the discipline, order, and ethical standards of Type 1.

Embracing Discipline and Structure: The influence of Type 1 encourages Type 4 women to apply self-discipline and structure to their creative endeavors and personal goals. This shift allows them to transform their rich inner worlds into tangible outcomes, bringing their visions and ideals into reality.

Pursuing Integrity and Purpose: As Type 4 integrates towards Type 1, their search for identity and meaning is grounded in a deeper sense of purpose and a commitment to live in alignment with their values. This integration fosters a sense of integrity, where Type 4 women find fulfillment in being true to themselves while contributing to the greater good.

Cultivating Objectivity: The objectivity and critical thinking associated with Type 1 help Type 4 women gain perspective on their emotional responses, leading to more balanced and rational decision-making. This objectivity does not diminish their emotional depth but rather provides a framework for navigating their feelings with wisdom and clarity.

Disintegration with Type 2: Navigating the Waters of Stress and Neediness

Under stress, Type 4 women may find themselves moving along the path of disintegration towards Type 2, exhibiting behaviors characterized by the need for affection and validation from others. This shift can lead to challenges as Type 4s seek external validation for their sense of identity and worth.

Seeking Validation: In moments of disintegration, Type 4's longing for uniqueness and significance can manifest as an excessive need for love and appreciation from others. Recognizing this tendency allows Type 4 women to seek internal sources of validation and self-esteem, rather than relying on external affirmation.

Over-Identifying with Others' Needs: The move towards Type 2 can also see Type 4 women over-identifying with the needs and emotions of those around them, at the expense of their own well-being. Acknowledging this pattern encourages them to set healthy boundaries and prioritize self-care.

"Managing Your Wings for Growth"

For Type 4 women, the concept of wings within the Enneagram offers a fascinating lens through which to view personal development and growth. Understanding and managing the influences of both Wings 3 and 5 can be a transformative process, allowing Type 4s to harness the strengths and mitigate the challenges of these adjacent types. This chapter delves into strategies for effectively engaging with these wings to foster personal growth, emotional balance, and a deeper understanding of oneself, rooted in the ancient wisdom of the Enneagram.

Understanding the Dynamics of Wings

The wings of an Enneagram type serve as complementary forces that add depth and complexity to the core personality. For Type 4, the Achiever (Type 3) and the Investigator (Type 5) offer contrasting yet enriching perspectives and capabilities. By acknowledging the presence and influence of these wings, Type 4 women can access a broader spectrum of traits and behaviors to navigate life's challenges and opportunities.

Engaging with Wing 3 for Motivation and Self-Actualization

Wing 3 brings to Type 4 an energizing drive for achievement, efficiency, and recognition. Type 4 women can leverage this influence to set and pursue goals with greater determination and to present their creative visions to the world with confidence. Embracing the healthy aspects of Wing 3 involves:

Cultivating a balanced approach to ambition, where achievements are pursued not just for external validation but as expressions of authentic personal values.

Developing practical skills and a constructive mindset that complements their emotional depth and creativity.

Utilizing the motivational energy of Wing 3 to overcome periods of inertia or self-doubt, channeling their emotional intensity into productive action.

Harnessing Wing 5 for Depth and Insight

Wing 5 offers Type 4 a pathway to deeper knowledge, introspection, and a detached perspective on emotions. This influence can enhance Type 4's natural inclination toward introspection, enriching their inner life and creative expression. Engaging with Wing 5 productively involves:

Embracing curiosity and a love of learning to expand their understanding of the world and themselves, which can inform and deepen their creative endeavors.

Practicing objectivity in emotional matters, using the analytical strengths of Wing 5 to gain clarity and perspective on their feelings and experiences.

Valuing solitude and reflection as sources of strength and rejuvenation, allowing for a balanced engagement with their rich inner world without becoming overwhelmed.

Balancing the Wings for Holistic Growth

The journey for Type 4 women involves finding a dynamic balance between the qualities of Wings 3 and 5. This balance allows for a harmonious integration of ambition and introspection, action and reflection, ensuring that personal and creative growth is pursued with both passion and wisdom. Strategies for achieving this balance include:

Regular self-reflection to understand the current influence of each wing on their personality and behavior, identifying areas for growth and development.

Setting intentions that honor both the drive for achievement and the need for deep understanding, creating goals that reflect a synthesis of these desires.

Seeking out experiences and relationships that challenge them to grow beyond their comfort zone, encouraging the development of underutilized aspects of their wings.

Wings as Catalysts for Growth

For Type 4 women, the wings are not merely adjuncts to their personality but integral components of their journey toward self-realization and fulfillment. By consciously engaging with the qualities of both Wings 3 and 5, Type 4s can navigate their path with greater adaptability, resilience, and insight. This engagement fosters a rich and balanced approach to personal development, where creativity, emotion, and intellect intertwine to create a life of depth, meaning, and authenticity. The Enneagram, with its deep historical roots and comprehensive understanding of human nature, serves as a guide on this journey, illuminating the way toward a fuller, more integrated expression of the Type 4 personality.

Chapter 8

WORKBOOK

Did you love *The Woman of Enneagram 4: Love, Marriage, Success Edition*? Then you should read *The woman of Enneagram 3: Love marriage success edition*[1] by Maria Rondon!

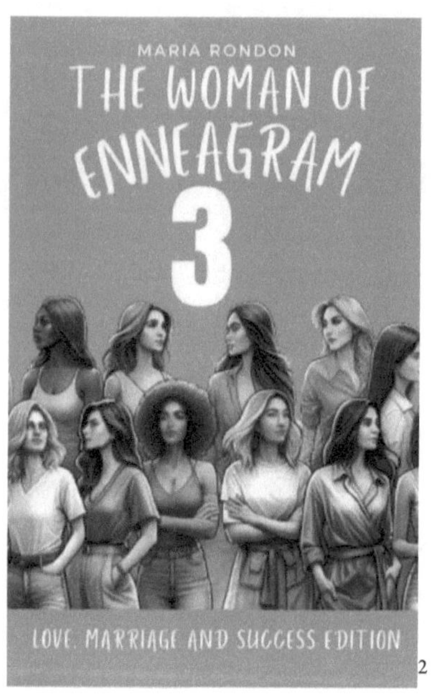

[2]

Enneagram Type 3 Woman Discover the transformative power of the Enneagram as a Type 3 woman. This life-changing book delivers invaluable insights into the core motivations, strengths, and growth opportunities for the Achiever personality type. As an Enneagram Type 3, you are driven by the desire to be successful, recognized, and admired in all areas of life. While these aspirations are motivating, they can also lead to a focus on external validation, adapting your persona to meet expectations, and a fear of failure. This book empowers you to embrace your authentic self while freeing yourself from limiting patterns. Through thought-provoking exercises and real-life examples, you'll

---

1. https://books2read.com/u/mK290y

2. https://books2read.com/u/mK290y

explore how the Enneagram influences your relationships (Enneagram in Love, Enneagram in Marriage), career, and personal development journey. Gain a deeper understanding of your motivations, learn to value your intrinsic worth over achievements, and develop self-acceptance and balance. If you aim to enhance your relationships, progress in your career, or simply live a more authentic and satisfying life, this book is an essential guide. It offers practical strategies and insights to help you leverage the strengths of your Type 3 personality while confronting your core fears and blind spots. Embark on this transformative journey today and begin a path of self-discovery, personal empowerment (Enneagram Empowerment), and significant growth (Enneagram for Personal Growth). Unlock your true potential as an Enneagram Type 3 woman and live with greater authenticity, purpose, and inner peace.

Also by Maria Rondon

Alzheimer
Alzheimer Guia para cuidadores

Enneagram For Women
The woman of Enneagram 1: Love Marriage Success Edition
The woman of enneagram 2
The woman of Enneagram 3: Love marriage success edition
The Woman of Enneagram 4: Love, Marriage, Success Edition
The woman of Enneagram 5: Love marriage success edition
The Woman of Enneagram 6: Love, Marriage, Success Edition
The woman of Enneagram 7: Love marriage success edition
The woman of Enneagram 8: Love marriage success edition
The woman of Enneagram 9: Love marriage success edition

LOA
El secreto para atraer tu alma gemela